What is taste?

Molly Aloian

🌳 Crabtree Publishing Company

www.crabtreebooks.com

Author
Molly Aloian

Publishing plan research and development
Sean Charlebois, Reagan Miller
Crabtree Publishing Company

Editorial director
Kathy Middleton

Editor
Crystal Sikkens

Proofreader
Kelly McNiven

Design
Samara Parent

Photo research
Samara Parent

Production coordinator
Margaret Amy Salter

Prepress technician
Kenneth J Wright

Print coordinator
Katherine Berti

Photographs
Thinkstock: page 4 (chilis)
All other images by Shutterstock

Library and Archives Canada Cataloguing in Publication

Aloian, Molly
        What is taste? / Molly Aloian.

(Senses close-up)
Includes index.
Issued also in electronic format.
ISBN 978-0-7787-0967-1 (bound).--ISBN 978-0-7787-0972-5 (pbk.)

        1. Taste--Juvenile literature. I. Title. II. Series: Senses close-up

QP456.A56 2013   j612.8'7   C2013-901422-5

Library of Congress Cataloging-in-Publication Data

Aloian, Molly.
        What is taste? / Molly Aloian.
            pages cm. -- (Senses close-up)
        Audience: 5-8.
        Audience: K to Grade 3.
        Includes index.
        ISBN 978-0-7787-0967-1 (reinforced library binding) -- ISBN 978-0-7787-
0972-5 (pbk.) -- ISBN 978-1-4271-9289-9 (electronic pdf) -- ISBN 978-1-4271-
9213-4 (electronic html)
        1. Taste--Juvenile literature. 2. Senses and sensation--Juvenile literature. 3.
Smell--Juvenile literature. I. Title.

QP456.A444 2013
612.8'7--dc23
                                                2013007631

Crabtree Publishing Company

www.crabtreebooks.com   1-800-387-7650

Printed in the U.S.A./042013/SX20130306

Published in Canada
Crabtree Publishing
616 Welland Ave.
St. Catharines, Ontario
L2M 5V6

Published in the United States
Crabtree Publishing
PMB 59051
350 Fifth Avenue, 59th Floor
New York, New York 10118

Published in the United Kingdom
Crabtree Publishing
Maritime House
Basin Road North, Hove
BN41 1WR

Published in Australia
Crabtree Publishing
3 Charles Street
Coburg North
VIC 3058

Contents

Your sense of taste

Taste is one of your five main senses. Your other four senses are touch, sight, hearing, and smell. You use all of your senses every day. Your senses help you learn about the world around you.

What do you think?

Name the five senses. What senses are you using to read this book?

Tasting food

Your sense of taste allows you to enjoy all kinds of foods and flavors. You can taste salty potato chips and popcorn or sweet cherries and apples. You can also taste sour lemons and spicy hot peppers.

hot peppers

5

Taste and smell

Your sense of taste works together with your sense of smell. You taste with your tongue, but a lot of what you taste comes from your sense of smell. The airway that you use to breathe is connected to both your nose and mouth. So as you eat, you breathe through your nose and smell your food.

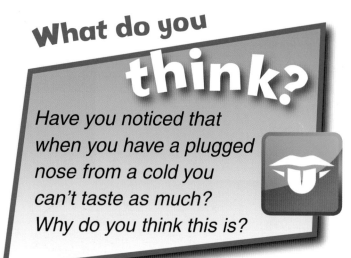

What do you think?

Have you noticed that when you have a plugged nose from a cold you can't taste as much? Why do you think this is?

Try pinching your nose when taking medicine you don't like.

6

Working together

The words "sweet," "sour," and "bitter" describe different tastes. These words also describe smells. This is because your senses of taste and smell work together to tell you what food tastes like.

Tongues and taste buds

You taste food inside your mouth. There are thousands of **taste buds** on your tongue and on the roof of your mouth. Taste buds are too small for you to see, but they are all over your tongue. There are taste **receptors** inside each taste bud.

Saliva in your mouth

Your tongue must be wet in order to taste. You have **saliva** in your mouth that keeps your tongue wet all of the time. Saliva helps you taste and helps break down the food that you eat.

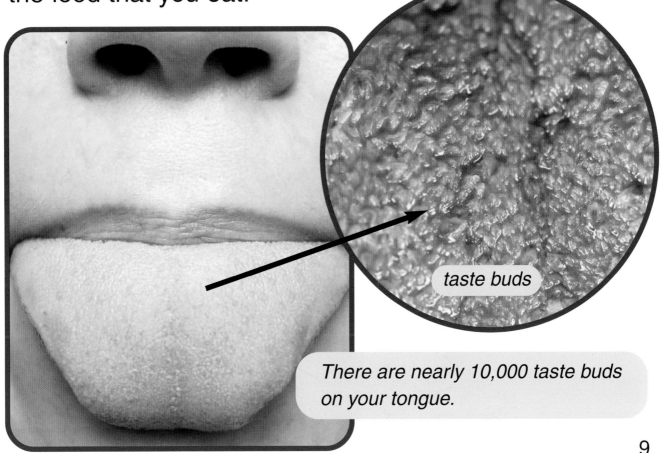

taste buds

There are nearly 10,000 taste buds on your tongue.

How do you taste?

When you put food in your mouth, your tongue feels if the food is hard or soft, hot or cold. The saliva in your mouth helps breaks down the food. Chemicals in the food then enter your taste buds.

Sending messages

Your taste receptors then send messages to your brain about how the food tastes. You can then decide what tastes good or bad to you. Your brain remembers many different tastes.

What do you think?

What foods have you tried that taste good to you? What foods do you think taste bad? How do you know without eating them?

Kinds of tastes

There are four main kinds of tastes. They are salty, sweet, sour, and bitter. Some scientists believe that all of the tongue's taste buds taste salty, sweet, sour, and bitter.

Different areas

Other scientists believe there are six areas on the tongue that sense different tastes. The taste buds at the back of your tongue taste bitter foods. Sour and salty are tasted in two areas on either side of your tongue. Sweet is tasted at the front on the tip of your tongue.

What do you think?

If our tongue tastes food in different areas, where on your tongue would you taste honey?

bitter

salty

sour

sweet

Tasting helps you

Your sense of taste helps you enjoy all kinds of foods. You can taste hundreds of flavors and enjoy eating many different foods. Your body needs a variety of healthy foods to grow and stay strong.

What do you think?

Think about the foods you ate today. Which of the four tastes were your foods?

Staying safe

Your sense of taste also protects you from eating rotten foods or **poisonous** things. Eating these things can make you sick. When you taste something that is not safe to eat or drink, your brain tells you to spit it out.

rotten apples

Taste lets you learn about your food before you swallow it.

Animals taste, too

Just like people, animals use their sense of taste all the time. A rabbit has about 17,000 taste buds on its tongue. It uses them to taste grass and other plants. Other animals taste with other body parts. For example, fish have taste buds in their mouths and also on their skin.

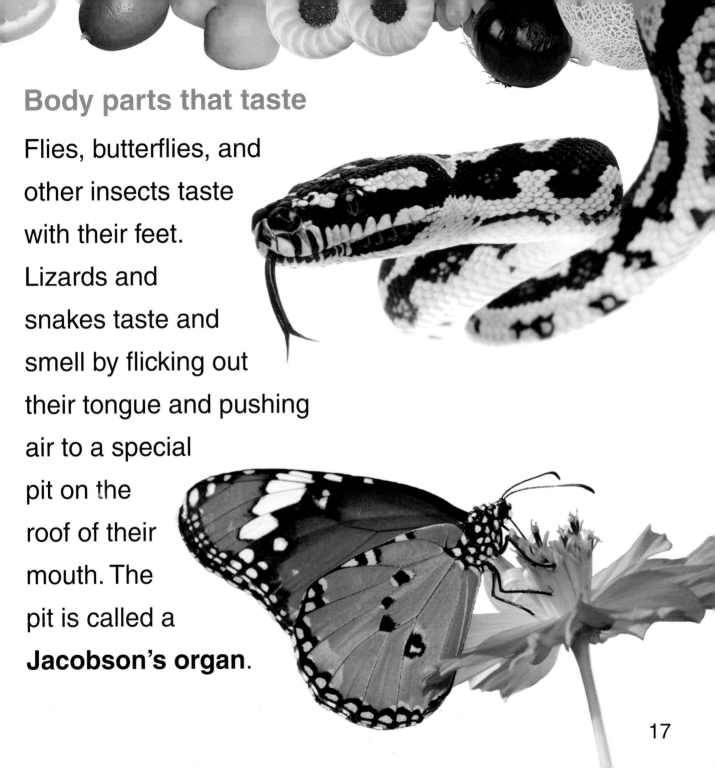

Body parts that taste

Flies, butterflies, and other insects taste with their feet. Lizards and snakes taste and smell by flicking out their tongue and pushing air to a special pit on the roof of their mouth. The pit is called a **Jacobson's organ**.

Did you know?

Babies have more taste buds than adults. They lose some of their taste buds as they get older. Adults have about 10,000 taste buds. As you get older, your taste buds die. Some older people only have about 5,000 taste buds left.

Swimming in saliva

If you think about eating something you love, your mouth starts making saliva right away. It is getting ready to taste your food. In your lifetime, your body will make enough saliva to fill a swimming pool!

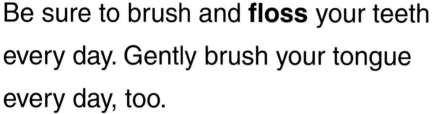

Be careful

It is important to take care of your sense of taste.
Keep sharp objects away from your tongue.
Be sure to brush and **floss** your teeth
every day. Gently brush your tongue
every day, too.

*dental
floss*

Tasting tips

Do not eat food that is very hot. You could burn your tongue and damage your taste buds. Do not taste or smell unfamiliar things, especially when you are sick with a cold. Being sick can lessen your ability to taste and smell things.

Be sure to let hot soup or stew cool before you eat it.

Taste test

Your senses of taste and smell work together when you eat. This activity will test how your sense of taste is affected when you cannot smell. You will need:

A slice of pear

A blindfold

A slice of apple

Blindfold a friend and ask him or her to plug their nose. Have your friend taste the pear slice and apple slice.

Can she or he tell the difference between the two slices?
How does not being able to smell affect the sense of taste?
How does not being able to see affect the sense of taste?

Learning more

Books

What is Taste? (Lightning Bolt Books: Your Amazing Senses)
by Jennifer Boothroyd. Lerner Publications, 2009.

Tasting and Smelling (Sparklers Senses) by Katie Dicker.
M. Evans and Company, 2011.

Tastes Good! (Let's Start Science) by Sally Hewitt.
Crabtree Publishing Company, 2008.

My Senses Help Me (My World) by Bobbie Kalman.
Crabtree Publishing Company, 2010.

Websites

The Sense of Taste
www.wisc-online.com/Objects/ViewObject.aspx?ID=AP14104

All About Your Senses: Experiments to Try
http://kidshealth.org/kid/closet/experiments/experiment_main.html

Sid the Science Kid
http://pbskids.org/sid/isense.html

What Are Taste Buds
http://kidshealth.org/kid/talk/qa/taste_buds.html

Words to know

floss (flaws) verb To use dental floss to clean between your teeth

Jacobson's organ (JEY-kuhb-suh-nz AWR-guh-n) noun An organ used for taste and smell found on the roof of the mouth of some reptiles

poisonous (POI-zuh-nuh-us) adjective Describing something that is dangerous or harmful

receptors (ri-SEP-ters) noun The parts of your body that receive messages and send them to your nerves and brain

saliva (suh-LAHY-vuh) noun Special liquid inside your mouth that helps you taste, swallow, and break down food

taste buds (teyst buhds) noun Very tiny parts of your tongue that let you taste things

A noun is a person, place, or thing. An adjective is a word that tells you what something is like. A verb is an action word that tells you what someone or something does.

Index

24